KOREAN
REUNIFICATION DAEBAK

KOREAN REUNIFICATION DAEBAK

Chang-min Shinn

KOREAN REUNIFICATION DAEBAK

"Daebak" is a Korean exclamatory expression for
an awesome and successful outcome.

Table of Contents

Endorsement

Even after the 2012 publication of his book, "Reunification is a Daebak,", Professor Chang-min Shinn has continued to write more: "Reunification is a Blessing" and "Reunification brings immense prosperity," and others. Along this path of tireless writings, Shinn has also engaged himself in further promotion and advocacy of the "Daebak theory" through various channels of lectures, seminars, interviews, and Facebook. He has done these whenever and wherever an opportunity arose. I am confident that Professor Shinn's efforts have not been in vain. Various opinions from a decade ago about reunification are now converging along the vision, direction, and the narratives of the Daebak theory.

Only about a decade ago, prevalent concern on reunification was that "the cost of achieving South-North Korean reunification is too burdensome or even impossible for us to bear." Today, we hear people saying, "Who doesn't know that reunification will be a Daebak?"

Following the framework of the Daebak theory, we must all recognize that the benefits will improve the living conditions and standards of both South and North Korean people. North Korean people must come to understand the realities of the outside world and agree with the humane and economic intentions of the Daebak theory. By following the Reunification Daebak theory, per capita income of all citizens in a unified Korea can rise to become one of the top two in the world, realizing a centuries-old dream of a prosperous and strong nation that can become a model for the world. The governing principles of unified One Korea will be liberal democracy, rule of law, and free-market economy.

I enthusiastically welcome President Yoon Suk-yeol's adoption of a reunification doctrine. In commemorative speech on the 79th Anniversary of Korea's liberation, President of the Republic of Korea declared that this doctrine would become government policy. The vision articulated by President Yoon is analogous to the goal presented in Shinn's Reunification Daebak Theory. The Yoon Administration has made a historic decision and seems poised to actively pursue it. I am thrilled! Thank you, President Yoon Suk-yeol! You are doing a wonderful job!

Shinn's concept of "voluntary reunification" suggests that North Korean people, who have been suffering under the tyrannical regime that has forced the absolute loyalty to the supreme leader and self-reliance above all, will initiate a "Mokran Revolution" and actively join the South's system of liberal democracy, market economy, and the rule of law, thereby achieving reunification. Although President Yoon's speech did not mention voluntary reunification, it is consistent with this concept.

I want more people to read Shinn's new book and support the vision and direction of Daebak. Day when a unified Korea will emerge to accomplish the great cause of Daebak may come sooner than we think. We must now get ready to move together toward the great cause of Daebak.

Jai-Poong RYU

Founder & President, One Korea Foundation

Professor Emeritus, Loyola University Maryland

Prologue

I. A book with the rather flippant title, 'Reunification is a daebak,' was published, and a year and a half later, at a press conference, President Park Geun-hye declared, "Reunification is a Daebak. I believe that.' This marked a dramatic shift in public sentiment, which had previously been burdened by the costs of reunification. Indeed, it was a seismic event. While there had been a growing sentiment that reunification was a national aspiration, a significant portion of the public, around 53%, remained hesitant due to the financial burden. However, when President Park made her 'Reunification is a daebak' remark at a New Year's press conference in 2014, public enthusiasm for reunification soared to an astonishing 82.6%.

The 'reunification daebak' narrative seemed to gain momentum with a series of positive developments under President Park, including the Dresden Declaration and the establishment of the National Reunification Advisory Council. However, this nascent momentum was derailed by the Sewol Ferry disaster. With the advent of the Moon Jae-in administration and its apparent leaning towards a lower-level federal system, akin to the communist ideology espoused by his revered figure, Shin Young-bok, the driving force behind the reunification daebak seemed to have completely evaporated.

We must revive our aspiration for a reunification daebak and elect a new president who is committed to achieving reunification. Together, we should actively work towards accelerating the process of reunification.

II. Some have argued that reunification would be a bust rather than a daebak, questioning who would truly benefit from it. However, there is essentially only one path to achieving a successful reunification. Let's delve deeper into the reality of the reunification daebak concept.

When we examine the underlying causes of Korea's various challenges, we invariably encounter the reality of our divided nation.

The North, clinging to its regime, is unable to provide for its people while prioritizing the Kim family's dynastic rule.

The Kim family is desperately clinging to their hereditary dictatorship. North Koreans live in fear of their superiors and face severe food shortages. Basic human rights are a distant dream for them.

It's good that the South has chosen the basic structure of liberal democracy and a market economy. However, we live in frustration, as we are constantly hindered by the divided state of the South and North, and are unable to make strides in vibrant development. Recently, it is said that the economy is difficult, and jobs are a problem. In fact, the ultimate and radical breakthrough to all these problems can be found in the permanent and fundamental solution of South-North reunification.

Without reunification, we cannot properly do anything well. This is true for economic problems, employment issues, and all general social problems, including human rights issues. It is impossible for all our people to live prosperous and dignified lives without reunification. Why must we live in such tension, unable to see even a step ahead? Can we continue like this for ten thousand years? To overcome this, both the South and the North must achieve reunification, even if it means paying a price.

In conclusion, the most desirable solution is for both South and North Korea to embrace the 'reunification daebak' framework. By achieving reunification and successfully implementing the 'reunification daebak' concept, we can resolve all our problems.

Both South and North Korea sing the song "Our Desire is Reunification." Yet, it now sounds like an empty, hollow tune that no longer feels real. So, what have we done in the 80 years since liberation and division? While we have paid lip service to reunification, neither the South nor the North has taken a single concrete step towards it. After President Lee Syng-man's goal of northward advance and Park Geun-hye's initial strides towards a "reunification daebak," Moon Jae-in, a man with leftist ideology, came to power and threw the nation into chaos. As soon as Moon became president, a Japanese media outlet directly called him a communist. However, the public simply ignored it.

Looking back, North Korea claimed to seek a confederation, but as the economic disparity between the South and North widened, Kim Il-sung declared in his 1991 New Year's address, "We don't want a reunification where we are eaten up." Meaning, he no longer had the power to absorb the South, so he simply wanted to avoid being absorbed. I believe this was an expression of giving up on reunification. Despite this, why did the Kim family, from Kim Jong-il to Kim Jong-un, continue to pay lip service to reunification? It's because they needed to give the North Korean people something to hope for in order to rally their support, but they had no other viable options. With nothing to offer and barely enough to eat, they could only cling to the hope of reunification. For them, reunification was merely a slogan to maintain internal cohesion.

Now, Kim Jong-un has even discarded this pretense, declaring that South Koreans are not of the same blood and that reunification is not a goal but simply a matter of hostile relations.

Given the global collapse of communist regimes in the last century, the Kim family must surely understand the futility of the proposed Koryo Confederal System under Kim Il-sung.

Concurrently, South Korean public sentiment has increasingly viewed reunification as an encumbrance rather than a gain. The enormous anticipated costs of reunification have led many South Koreans to perceive it as a financial burden.

To counteract this short-sighted perspective, it was imperative to emphasize the substantial benefits of reunification. After extensive research, I compiled a document outlining the vast advantages of reunification and uploaded it to the National Assembly Budget Committee's homepage in August 2007. Building upon this foundation, I further developed these ideas into a book titled "Reunification is a Daebak," which was published in 2012.

In the dire circumstances of a divided Korea, let us examine our current reality. Are we facing economic challenges? Is there a shortage of jobs? It is crucial to recognize that reunification offers a fundamental solution to these problems, both in the short and long term.

In essence, whether we're looking at the economy or employment, reunification is the solution, both before and after it occurs. Why is this so?

Let's begin by examining the stabilization phase following reunification, the period after we successfully complete the reunification process.

To comprehend the post-reunification landscape, we must

conduct a concrete comparison between the costs associated with reunification and the benefits it will yield.

To put it succinctly, if we diligently adhere to the "reunification daebak" scenario, the per capita GDP of the entire Korean Peninsula ten years after reunification will soar to the second highest in the world, trailing only the United States, as depicted in Table 2. This will mark a completely unprecedented era in our nation's history, a veritable paradise. I've personally encountered numerous individuals, both domestically and internationally, who were unable to conceal their excitement upon first hearing this prospect.

The Status of a Unified Korea 10 Years After Achieving the "Reunification Daebak"

*Second in the world after the United States
among the G7 nations*

As shown in Table 1 below, a realistic assessment of the world's major economies, based on their GDP per capita in 2023 and estimated population in 2024, reveals the following.

Table 1: GDP per capita (2023) and Population Size of Major Countries

Country	GDP per capita (USD)	Population (thousands)
United States	81,585	341,693
Germany	52,739	84,119
United Kingdom	48,867	68,459
France	44,115	68,375
Japan	33,879	123,202
China (Reference)	12,666	1,416,043
South Korea	33,136	52,081
North Korea	1,107	26,299

Data Source: Economic Statistics System 2024 by Bank of Korea and populations of countries by CIA The World Factbook 2024

If unified Korea successfully operates its economy for 10 years according to the "reunification daebak" scenario, it will reap enormous benefits that are difficult to fully express with words. For example, if reunification occurs when South Korea's GDP per capita is around $33,000, and if the economy grows at a rate of 10.22% annually for the next 10 years, the GDP per capita will reach nearly $80,000. During this period, North Korea's GDP per capita will grow at half the rate of South Korea. If the economies of the South and North are fully integrated under these conditions, the average GDP per capita of a unified Korea will exceed $69,000, as shown in Table 2. This would be a truly remarkable achievement.

Table 2: Projected GDP per Capita of G7 Countries

10 Years After Korean Reunification

Country	Projected GDP per Capita 10 Years After Korean Reunification (USD)
United States	150,468
Unified Korea	69,254*
United Kingdom	61,817
Germany	59,344
France	44,461
Japan	33,879
China*	12,666* (*2022)

Let's compare this with the projected changes in the GDP per capita of major countries shown in Table 1. Based on Table 1, by applying the average growth rate of each country over the past 11 years, and if Korean reunification occurs in 2029, the projected GDP per capita of each country 10 years later is summarized in Table 2.

If the average GDP per capita of a unified Korea reaches approximately $69,000, it would surpass the levels of major countries such as the UK, Germany, France, and Japan, placing it second only to the United States. This would make our entry into the G7 a non-issue.

As a large-scale economy ranked second in the world, this might sound somewhat unrealistic now. However, if we accept these estimates based on facts and if the entire nation unites and strives towards this goal, we can fully achieve it.

This is not a baseless claim because, as we will see below, it is grounded in solid effective demand in macroeconomics. Recently, the term "reunification daebak" has been circulating, but merely discussing it in that way will not lead to a reunification daebak.

The scenarios presented by Goldman Sachs, individuals close to President Park Geun-hye's reunification preparatory committee, the members of Financial Services Commission at the time, and Jim Rogers are insufficient to achieve the daebak and are merely empty words. More details will be provided sequentially later.

Background Data for Estimation

Data Source: Economic Statistics System 2024 and Conversion by Bank of Korea, KOSIS National Statistical Portal 2024
  South Korea GDP: US$ 1,798.6 billion in 2023
  South Korea GDP per capita: US$ 33,136 in 2023
  North Korea GDP per capita: US$ 1,107 in 2023
  Population: North Korea 25.66 million in 2023, South Korea 51.628 million in 2023

Assumptions Used for Rough Estimation of Reunification Costs
  1. Population growth rate: South Korea 0.5%, North Korea 0.5%
  2. If reunification occurs in 2029, South Korea's GDP will be 2.4 times that of 2023 in 10 years, North Korea's growth rate without reunification: 1.0165%
  3. Capital output ratio: 2.174 (based on 2015 statistics)
  4. Depreciation rate of physical capital: 6.7%

Chapter 02

A New Dawn for Our Nation

Throughout our long history, our ancestors have fundamentally loved peace and pursued the noble ideal of 'Hongik Ingan'[1].

To realize this ideal, strength is essentially required. In the past, that strength might have been military power. In the present, economic power forms the basis of that strength. However, we have not yet experienced sustained, powerful strength.

Once we successfully achieve the reunification daebak and raise the living standards of our people, creating a groundbreaking new nation that surpasses the miracle on the Han River, the situation will change.

We desire Korean reunification. South Koreans do not seek reunification to exploit North Koreans' cheap labor or the North's abundant mineral resources. We want North Koreans to understand that reunification will lead to prosperity for both the South and the North. Furthermore, we are not merely striving for the well-being of the South and the North. We are of the same bloodline, sharing a common ancestry that dates back thousands of years to Central Asia. Over thousands of years, we have formed

---

[1] The concept of Hongik Ingan, which means "broadly benefiting humanity," has been a central part of Korean culture for centuries.

various states and even waged wars against each other. However, we are all descendants of the same ancestral lineage, the people of Korea.

If we, as a unified Korean people, can achieve the reunification daebak and contribute to global peace and prosperity, we will acquire new strength and capabilities. With this newfound power, we will not only strive for the betterment of our own people but also establish a global system based on Hongik Ingan, a philosophy of benefiting all humanity. This will enable us to realize the grand goal of extending the benefits of our civilization to people around the world.

We envision a future where countries worldwide aspire to follow Korea's example of development, a vision we call the 'K-Dream.' Soon, a unified Korea will take the lead in creating a new world of peace and prosperity.

Once our per capita income ranks second in the world, next to the United States, we will enter a completely new chapter in our history. For five millennia, our people have suffered countless hardships caught between the continental and maritime powers. When the continent was powerful, hundreds of thousands of our women were abducted. When the maritime powers rose, our land was devastated, and we were eventually colonized. We have been pushed around by the continent and battered by the sea. However, if we faithfully follow the blueprint laid out for the reunification daebak, the situation will be completely reversed. Instead of being victimized, our people will rise to prominence on the world stage. We will no longer be pushed around by the continent or the sea; instead, we will extend our influence in both directions. Isn't this a truly exhilarating and wonderful prospect? This is the future that awaits our people.

Should we merely seek retribution for the past injustices we have suffered? No, that is not the way. Instead, we should rediscover our ancestral roots that trace back to Central Asia and spread out across the vast expanse of the world. By reviving the unique spirit of Hongik Ingan among our people, we can inspire the world to embrace this ideal. Ultimately, the fruits of our reunification will become a shared goal for all people, and the 'K-Dream' will become a universal aspiration.

Ultimately, we will create a world where all humanity benefits, starting with our own people who share the ancestral philosophy of Hongik Ingan. Based on this, Korea will become the center of a world where all nations aspire to realize the 'K-Dream.' As a result, Korea will be the driving force and the central figure in ensuring the continuous development of human civilization. I wish we aspire to lead a community of people who are dedicated to serving humanity.

As we ascend to the ranks of the world's leading nations through the completion of the reunification daebak, there is something we must do. It is to properly find our original roots. We believe that the first step is to find our roots and use them as a starting point to practically spread the world of Hongik Ingan for the benefit of all our people.

Our ancestors were bound by myths, a result of the schemes of the continental and maritime powers.

How can we believe that a bear became human by eating garlic just a few thousand years ago, and how can we believe that a king was born from an egg only a few thousand years ago?

Japan could not accept that its history was shorter than Korea's. This is because they could not tolerate the fact that they were superior to us but had a shorter history. So, when Japan was stronger than us, Koreans learned from the Japanese and Korean scholars who learned history from the Japanese during that period cut off their own country's history.

Meanwhile, during the Han Dynasty, China, with its strong national power, referred to people outside its borders as barbarians, such as the Dongyi people. This was only about 2,000 years ago. Here, "Dongyi" means barbarians from east of China.

However, the history of our Central Asian people is older than that of the Han Chinese in the Yellow River Basin. This is clearly stated in Sim Baek-gang's book, "China was once a part of Korea." The recent publication of the book "History of Goguryeo in China" during the Northeast Project is merely their beautification project. Originating in Central Asia and moving southeast through Mongolia, Manchuria, the three northeastern provinces of China, and the Russian Far East have a longer history than the Han Chinese in the Yellow River Basin. Despite this, China claims that Goguryeo and Balhae were originally theirs. That's why you can't even take pictures at the old site of Balhae.

China has made attempts to claim Korean history as part of its own through projects like the Northeast Project and publications such as "History of Goguryeo in China." However, historical evidence, as demonstrated by Dr. Sim Baek-gang, clearly shows that Korean history predates Chinese history.

Upon achieving reunification daebak, our priority should be to establish a world based on Hongik Ingan, starting with our ancestral roots. We should extend a helping hand to the northeastern part of China and parts of Japan, bringing them under the sphere of Hongik Ingan, and become a friend to countries worldwide pursuing the K-Dream.

Fundamental Condition and Four Crucial Conditions for Achieving a Reunification Daebak

The immense benefits of reunification cannot be automatically acquired by achieving reunification. At least the following fundamental condition and four crucial conditions must be met.

I. Fundamental Condition

If we want to achieve the reunification daebak, it is only possible when the fundamental condition is met at the root of the system.

To put it simply, it is crucial to remember that the reunification daebak can only be achieved in a situation where a system of liberal democracy, market economy, and the rule of law is established.

Does this seem easy? In a situation mixed with imperfect socialism or communism, the path to the reunification daebak cannot be properly developed. In the current Korean situation, which is contaminated in many ways, it is not that simple. We must be particularly aware of this fundamental condition and take steps to correct them.

II. Four Crucial Conditions

Before discussing the four crucial conditions, I want to emphasize a very important point. These are not easy tasks.

Let's recall a famous saying by Chairman of Hyundai, Jeong Joo-young.

"Have you tried?"

Whenever he assigned a task, especially a challenging one, and his subordinates responded with, "Mr. Chairman, it's too difficult, it won't work," he would simply ask, "Have you tried?"

If something seems difficult, you should make it happen. If you think that it is difficult and impossible, it is clear that it will not be accomplished. Chairman Jeong, with this spirit of breakthrough, made things that ordinary people cannot imagine, and he made a great contribution to the development of the country by establishing a large corporation.

To achieve reunification and successfully complete the reunification daebak, we must keep in mind that we must successfully prepare all four crucial conditions below and successfully implement them no matter what. Each one is difficult and arduous. However, if there is a problem with any one of them, even if reunification is achieved, the South and the North may sink together, embracing each other, rather than making a daebak.

Therefore, we must be prepared to properly prepare and operate these crucial conditions no matter what.

Since this book is in summary form, it is difficult to describe in detail how to meet these crucial conditions. (The main parts of the solutions are described in the books "Reunification is a Daebak" published in 2012, 2015, and 2017.) In any case, if it doesn't work out, make it done!

If we look at the policies that are fundamentally key to reducing the cost of reunification and maximizing the economic benefits from reunification, they are centered around the separate management of the South and the North in the economic sector, the Buy

Korean Products Policy, temporary arms reduction, compensation for land securities instead of returning land in kind to the original owners of North Korean land, and continued maintenance of the nationalization of real estate such as North Korean land for the 10 years after reunification.

In order to smoothly implement these policies, the public's accurate perception of reality, the formation of a consensus on countermeasures, and specific preparations for each of them must be made at the right time and in detail.

1) For the first 10 years after reunification, North Korea should be managed separately in terms of economics.

During the 10-year period of adjusting the income gap between the South and the North, we should not take the approach of helping North Korean residents live off government transfers funded by South Korean taxes. Instead of giving them fish, we should teach them how to fish by providing them with fishing equipment and skills. Creating conditions for North Korean residents to stand on their own feet will minimize the burden on South Korean citizens. This is the best way to reduce the cost of reunification.

If we follow the German model of immediately mixing everything together after reunification and providing social security benefits, we must first realize that this is simply beyond our capabilities. In reality, the cost of reunification would more than double, and tax burdens alone would jump a whopping eight times over a long period. It's not just a simple matter of doubling.

The reason for separate management of the economy for 10 years is not to discriminate against or control North Korean residents at the time of reunification. Rather, it is to create conditions for North Korean residents to maintain their self-esteem and become self-reliant. Our people are hard-working and have the ability to live well. By doing it this way, we can efficiently and rapidly improve the income and living standards of all North Korean residents in a short period of time.

Separate management is necessary because of the following problems and advantages.

First, it is observed that a planned economy operates more efficiently than a free market economy in the early stages of economic development. A planned economy is ideal for rapidly raising the significantly underdeveloped North Korean economy to a certain level.

Second, North Korean residents have lived in isolation for a very long time. It would require excessive effort to help each of them adapt to a new environment individually. In fact, full adaptation in all aspects may require as much time as the divided period. In this situation, it would be more efficient to group those with similar problems together and provide them with collective adaptation training and daily living training. Furthermore, due to the socialist nature of the society, most of them have significantly lower productivity. If they were to go through individual retraining processes for production activities, it would be a tremendous waste.

Third, once reunification occurs and people from both regions work together without regional distinctions, demands for equal pay for equal work will immediately arise. However, the productivity gap between the South and the North is also a problem. Moreover, the total amount of wages and salaries paid would become excessively high, which is a realistic problem considering the burden of reunification costs. Paying excessively high wages, as in Germany, would harm North Korean workers. That is, their products, with high prices relative to their quality, would not sell well. As a result, factories would close, leading to unemployment. During the income adjustment period, it is desirable for North Korean workers to receive wages commensurate with their productivity, both in terms of the overall burden on society and their own interests.

Fourth, if people from the South and North are immediately mixed without distinction, the productivity gap will be easily exposed. A significant income gap will follow. Naturally, a clear distinction will arise between a "first-class" citizen group and a "third class" citizen group. As a result, unexpected discrimination and social conflict will arise.

Fifth, it is advisable to prohibit the formation of labor unions in North Korea during the 10-year period of separate management. Given the significant productivity gap and the fact that North Koreans are unfamiliar with the new system, excessive demands could easily develop, acting as a major obstacle to the overall economy.

All these problems can be minimized through separate management.

In short, separate management can avoid inefficiencies, reduce reunification costs, and fundamentally prevent the occurrence of economic risks and unnecessary social conflicts.

Thus, separate management is essential for the first 10 years after reunification. Without it, successful reunification would simply become impossible.

However, many people question whether North and South separate management is possible. Nevertheless, separate management must be established based on the following framework.

First, there is a pull effect. The reason why there is a force pulling people towards their original residence is that the economy starts to move, and jobs are created in the vicinity of their original residence, so there is no need to wander to unfamiliar places shrouded in uncertainty.

Second, simultaneously, a push effect can be applied to prevent people from going outside. North Korean residents have lived in a society without freedom of residence for over half a century. It is not new for them to be continuously controlled by law from the beginning in the same way.

Third, if necessities such as food, clothing, and medicine, along with a minimum living allowance, are provided only to North Korean residents who remain in their original regions from immediately after reunification, this will serve as a very strong deterrent in reality.

2) *Buy Korean Products Policy*

The "Buy Korean Products Policy" is a crucial policy that can significantly maximize the benefits of reunification during the South-North income adjustment period, while simultaneously contributing to reducing and securing reunification costs. I would like to point out that the biggest secret to the reunification daebak lies here. The result of developing this policy is reminiscent of the story of Columbus' egg. Although it may seem insignificant once it is done, it is actually a critically important part. The United States has also adopted a "Buy American" policy when necessary. This time, as we are in a situation where we are successfully completing reunification, it is necessary to seek understanding and cooperation from major powers such as the United States, Japan, China, and Russia.

To raise the North Korean income level to half of South Korea's within 10 years, real capital equivalent to approximately 7% of South Korea's GDP must be invested in the North Korean region each year. We cannot simply leave this all to the international market. It is essential for South Korea to oversee and provide everything.

Therefore, before reunification, it is crucial to make our special circumstances understood by surrounding major powers and to secure the necessary cooperation when the critical opportunity arises. After reunification, it is not that we will ask them for any material aid. It is simply for them to watch as we develop and solve problems on our own. As a result, at least 80% of the real capital equivalent to 7% of South Korea's GDP should be produced and procured in South Korea. This means increasing real production by 5.6% of South Korea's GDP. Based on this effective demand, the South Korean economy can enter a period of rapid economic growth.

I sometimes see some people who are very skeptical about whether such a "Buy Korean Products Policy" is possible. To this end, we can first make it possible through domestic regulations and technical processing methods. In addition, before reunification, we need to continuously carry out preliminary work to broaden mutual understanding by informing social leaders of major countries who will be future stakeholders about our circumstances and plans. It is too late to seek the understanding of surrounding major powers when our interests become intertwined on the verge of reunification.

By adding the production increase of 1.92% resulting from the partial industrialization of the military and the trend growth potential of 2.7% to the production increase of 5.6% of the gross national product due to the Buy Korean Products Policy, the South Korean economy will achieve a phenomenal economic growth of 10.22% annually for 10 years after reunification, leaping to the level of a first-class advanced country. This is a realistic scenario based on overall effective demand.

If we simply compare the economic gains and losses in terms of reunification costs, we find that the cost of division is greater than the cost of reunification, leading to the conclusion that reunification is much better than not doing so. In fact, if we can go beyond overcoming economic recession and achieve ground-breaking economic growth, who would refuse reunification? We can create a reunification that makes money rather than spends money.

In this way, if companies that gain net profits due to special circumstances that arise in special situations pay a portion of them as special contributions rather than general taxes, some of the consumable costs, such as emergency management costs and costs for unifying various systems, can be used to cover the types of reunification costs mentioned above.

3) *Temporary Military Spending Reduction*

Given the need to finance the enormous reunification costs during the South-North income adjustment period after reunification, it is desirable to keep military spending below 1% of GDP. Here again, the understanding and cooperation of major world powers such as the United States, China, Russia, and Japan are necessary. If this policy is feasible, approximately 2% of the 7% GDP reunification cost per year can be resolved over the 10 years after reunification.

Japan has maintained its Self-Defense Forces budget at around 1% of GDP for decades under the protection of the United States.

It is urgent for us to maintain our military spending at 1% of GDP for at least the first 10 years after reunification. We need to secure the cooperation of major powers such as the United States, Japan, China, and Russia to prevent anyone from militarily threatening us.

One might question whether such a temporary military spending reduction would be possible given the expected opposition from the South Korean military. However, I believe that this would not be a major problem in the following context.

First, South Korean professional soldiers will continue to maintain their respective positions as professional soldiers even after reunification. The lower structure of the military will primarily consist of young people from the North, who have relatively low productivity at the time of reunification.

Second, South Korean young people who are freed from military service during this process can either immediately work at the industry or continue their studies to improve their future productivity. Young people no longer need to be forcibly into military service.

Third, in the process of reorganizing the military, it is desirable to discharge all troops above the North's key soldiers in the past and have them engage in production after going through an industrial training process.

Fourth, until the military organization takes root in the North for a considerable period after reunification, the return of most of the South's reserve generals and officers to active duty and service will be the fastest way to stabilize the military organization.

Fifth, given the long-standing ROK-US relationship, it is important to maintain cooperation so that the US military can be stationed in a unified Korea for as long as possible after the 10-year period of income adjustment between the South and the

North after reunification, as well as after that, if necessary, in consideration of convenience. In this case, the stationing location of the US military should not be in the form of moving northward from the time of reunification. This is because China could become unnecessarily sensitive.

Sixth, if a Northeast Asian security cooperation system such as the Commission on Security and Cooperation in Europe (CSCE) can be established during this process, it would be the icing on the cake.

4) Maintaining North Korean State Ownership of Land and Compensation with Land Value Securities

Instead of returning physical land to the original owners of land in the North after reunification, compensation in the form of land value securities, like those issued during the South Korean land reform in 1949, is the answer. Germany adopted a policy of returning physical land based on the simple principle of original ownership but was embroiled in as many as 2.2 million lawsuits at once. There is also the issue of equity with the land reform implemented in South Korea in the past.

In addition, the North Korean land system should continue to maintain state ownership as it has been. In the very long term, it is desirable to unify the entire country by unifying the South Korean land system with the North Korean state ownership system. It is preferable to unify with the North rather than the South in terms of the land system. This is a measure to compensate for the inherent weaknesses of the market economy.

It is important to continue with the current state ownership system for North Korean land after reunification. This is essential for successfully completing reunification without unnecessarily expanding reunification costs. If the state were to repurchase privatized land to expand social overhead capital facilities, it would require astronomical resources. Moreover, this measure is essential for the long-term development of the unified Korean economy and society. Land speculation caused by a limited amount of land should be considered a public enemy. This compensation for the shortcomings of the market economy system is only possible in Korea, where the North and South have been divided for a long time. This will allow us to implement one of the most exemplary market economic systems in the world.

** In addition to the above conditions, the area that we must pay special attention to before and after the reunification process of Korea is the strong Korea-US relations.*
South Korea barely survived the Korean War, which was on the verge of becoming communist, thanks to the decision of US President Truman and the help of the UN forces centered on the US military. After that, South Korea achieved the miracle on the Han River thanks to the outstanding achievements of President Park Chung-hee.

Now that Korea is entering the stage of reunification of the North and the South, which is a long-cherished wish of Korea, cooperation from the US is very important before and after reunification. Of course, I am talking about financial help from them.

From the US perspective, I hope that Korea's remarkable development is considered a very proud feat. Among the many countries that have received help from the US in world history, South Korea is the only one that has developed significantly and grown into a great country. This is an additional great achievement for the US to boast about on the world stage.

However, if Korea does not stop there and achieves reunification daebak and is reborn as a great country that has made a fortune from reunification, it will also be of great benefit to the US. Of course, there is an economic benefit that expands the scope of mutual benefits between Korea and the US through trade based on comparative advantage. However, realistically, in the position where the US is competing with China for global leadership, Korea's role is incomparable to that of any other country in the world. Therefore, the US does not need to obsess over the small economic gains it can gain by persuading North Korea's Kim Jong-un and making North Korea as prosperous as Vietnam.

If Korea is unified and the US and Korea continue to maintain a strong alliance, it will be like an American ally that far surpasses Japan in terms of the Chinese Communist Party emerging in eastern Asia. It will be a tremendous power for the US.

❄ *Appendix 1: Draft of Reunification Daebak Special Act*

(※ If reunification occurs suddenly, instead of being flustered or confused, it is desirable to immediately start working on the reunification daebak project based on the draft of this special act and to refine the specific details from that point on.)

(※ Caution: Discussions on a "Reunification Constitution" should take place after the 10-year period of South-North regional income growth adjustment according to the "Reunification Daebak Special Act" after reunification. This is because if the Reunification Constitution is prioritized, it will make it impossible to gradually adjust the income between the South and North regions.)

(Basis of the Law) The Reunification Daebak Special Act is based on the Constitution of the Republic of Korea before reunification.

In particular, its core essence is specifically summarized as a free democratic system, a market economic system, and the rule of law.

Communist or socialist elements that conflict with these core elements cannot be introduced.

(Purpose) The purpose of this special act is to ensure that the per capita income level of the North Korean region (hereinafter referred to as the North region) exceeds the South Korean level at the time of reunification in the shortest possible time, while at the same time achieving rapid economic growth in the South Korean region (hereinafter referred to as the South region) in this process. It is not a situation where one side makes unilateral sacrifices or benefits for the other.

(Government organization of the North region in a unified government)

For 10 years after reunification, in the process of significantly raising the income level of North Korean residents by completing the reunification daebak structure, a Second Prime Minister will be appointed to oversee all North Korean departments.

The Second Prime Minister will be responsible only to the President.

For the 10-year period during which the Reunification Daebak Special Act is applied, a separate second government ministry will be organized under the Second Prime Minister to oversee the North Korean region.

To achieve the purpose of this special act, the National Intelligence Service, the Ministry of National Defense, and related agencies, as well as the Legislative Affairs Commission, will remain as overall South-North coordinating bodies, overseeing both the South and North. However, the Ministry of Reunification will be abolished.

For national security, the department in charge of overseeing the North region under the National Intelligence Service will be generally within the framework of the National Intelligence Service, but its specific activities will be carried out independently.

As a result, for 10 years after reunification, each region of the South and North will generally maintain separate administrative and judicial organizations.

Chapter 1: Act on the Scope of Employable Areas for North Korean Residents Before Reunification

Article 1 [Purpose] The purpose of this Act is to specify the employable areas for North Korean residents after reunification.

Article 2 [Scope of Employment Areas] For 10 years after reunification, the employment area for North Korean residents shall be limited to within the pre-reunification North Korean region. Simple travel is not restricted. Job changes within the North Korean region are allowed for 10 years.

Article 3 [Place of Employment] The place of employment for North Korean residents shall be determined by the person in charge of the regional community center of the Second Ministry of the Interior and Safety within the guidelines of the Second Ministry of Economy and Finance, taking into account the individual's wishes and abilities to the maximum extent possible.

Article 4 [Regional Industrial Master Plan] This master plan shall be prepared in cooperation with the Second Ministry of Economy and Finance, the Second Ministry of Trade, Industry and Energy, the Second Ministry of SMEs and Startups, and the Second Ministry of Land, Infrastructure and Transport.

Article 5 [Government Subsidies] If it is necessary to provide state living allowances to North Korean residents immediately after reunification, they shall be limited to those who continuously reside in the North Korean region for 10 years after reunification.

Chapter 2: Act on the Buy Korea Policy

Article 1 [Purpose] The purpose of this Act is to stipulate that, in procuring physical capital necessary for the economic growth of the North Korean region, the principle is to use physical capital produced entirely in the South, except in cases where imports from overseas are indispensable.

Article 2 [Import] In cases where the procurement of physical capital from the South is unavoidably difficult, imports from overseas shall be permitted with the approval of the Second Ministry of Trade, Industry and Energy. Overseas imports should be kept to a minimum, preferably within 20% of the total South Korean GDP.

Chapter 3: Act on Compensation for Privately Owned Land in the North Korean Region Before Reunification

Article 1 [Purpose] The purpose of this Act is to definitively establish ownership of land in the North Korean region.

Article 2 [Ownership and Use Rights of Land in the North Korean Region] All land in the pre-reunification North Korean region shall continue to be state-owned property of the unified Republic of Korea. Land users shall have the right to use the land.

Article 3 [Land Compensation] In the case of all land in the North Korean region that was confiscated by the North Korean regime, compensation shall be paid in the form of land value securities at a level similar to that provided to landowners in South Korea under the Farmland Compensation Act of 1949, provided that the original land ownership certificate is possessed. Physical return of land will not be made.

Article 4 [Department in Charge of Land Compensation in the North Korean Region] The Second Ministry of Agriculture, Food and Rural Affairs, the Second Ministry of Land, Infrastructure and Transport, and the Second Ministry of Economy and Finance shall jointly establish compensation regulations based on the Farmland Compensation Act of 1949, which was implemented in South Korea, and carry out compensation for land in the North Korean region.

Chapter 4: Exchange Rate for North Korean Currency

Article 1 [Exchange] North Korean currency held by North Korean residents before reunification shall be exchanged for the currency of Republic of Korea based on its market purchasing power.

Article 2 [Non-Repayment of Foreign Debt] North Korean currency or bonds held by foreign countries shall be excluded from the exchange.

Article 3 [Illegal North Korean Currency] North Korean currency that the North Korean authorities provided to residents free of charge on the eve of reunification shall be excluded from the exchange.

Chapter 5: Restrictions During the Enforcement Period of this Special Act

Article 1 [Restriction on the Organization of Labor Unions and Other Civil Organizations] During the period of enforcement of this special law, the organization of all labor unions, including the Korean Confederation of Trade Unions, the Korean Confederation of Trade Unions, the Korean Press Union, the Korean Teachers and Education Workers Union, and the Public Officials Union, as well as any similar private organizations, in the northern region will be prohibited.

Article 2 [Complete Disbandment of All Military Organizations in the North Korean Region] All military organizations in the northern region shall be completely disbanded immediately upon reunification.

Article 3 [Non-existence of Assemblies at All Levels] During the enforcement period of this Special Act, no assemblies at all levels, including the National Assembly and local assemblies, shall exist.

Article 4 [Judicial System in the Northern Region] During the enforcement period of this Special Act, the judicial system in the northern region shall be a separate single-instance system.

Article 5 [Conversion and Restriction of the Conscription System in the Southern Region to a Volunteer System] After reunification, the conscription system in the southern region shall be converted to a volunteer system. During the enforcement of this Special Act, northern residents shall not be subject to any military service requirements.

Article 6 [Military Expenditure] During the enforcement of this Act after reunification, total military expenditure shall be limited to approximately 1% of the GDP of the unified Republic of Korea, subject to security cooperation with the United States and Japan.

(Regarding land ownership)*

Free-market economies inherently have several inherent flaws.

Particularly, in countries with limited land, a chronic disease of wealth polarization due to land speculation tends to appear prominently.

To mitigate this, it would be prudent to nationalize land over a long period, such as 50-70 years, while minimizing harm to innocent victims.

This book merely suggests a direction in this regard, leaving the actual coordination to future generations.

One of the important factors that allowed a reunified Korea to achieve a reunification daebak was that all the land in the North before reunification was continuously nationalized after the establishment of the North Korean government and the two Koreas were united.

Then, when the South and the North go to the same land system after achieving the reunification daebak, which side should we choose? As a result, it would be more desirable to unify with the North's nationalization system rather than the South's private ownership system regarding land.

One might question whether there is no problem in following the land nationalization form of China or North Korea, which are on the wrong path. However, the primary purpose of land nationalization in communist countries is, in fact, to use land as a powerful and important means of controlling the people. In contrast, the nationalization of land in a unified Korea is a means to overcome the inherent disadvantage of land speculation when adopting a free-market economy in a country with limited land, so it has a great advantage over other Western countries. It is a very big advantage that divided countries with different systems can obtain in the process of national reunification. Although being divided and alienated has a great disadvantage, this divided state has turned into an advantageous situation.

(※ North Koreans are expected to gain a significant advantage, particularly in the real estate sector after Korean reunification.)

Immediately following Korean reunification, the nationalization of land in the North will place northern residents in a significantly advantageous position regarding individual housing compared to southern residents. Due to the low construction costs and affordable land usage fees associated with state-owned land, northern residents will enjoy much more affordable housing options during the early stages of reunification.

Chapter 04

The Reunification Daebak is What Happens After Reunification.
Then What is The Path to Reunification?

After 80 years of division, I've concluded that the only viable path to reunification is through voluntary reunification based on Theory R.

Theory R, or The Strategies for Korean Reunification, is rooted in the late 20th century economist Jan Tinbergen's general policy theory, which posits that the number of policy instruments must at least equal the number of policy objectives. I applied this theory to the Korean Peninsula in 1994.

The crux of the matter is that the number of policy instruments must match the number of policy objectives in reunification policy.

In reality, there are two entities in North Korea: the regime and the people. Their goals are fundamentally different. The regime seeks to maintain its power, while the people aspire to a better life.

These goals are mutually exclusive. As long as Kim Jong-un maintains his communist kingdom, economic development and a decent life for the people will remain elusive.

Kim Jong-un and his regime will never willingly relinquish power.

Therefore, negotiating reunification with the regime is futile. Any negotiations would be merely for show.

To achieve reunification, we must approach the problem by

separating the regime from the people. This means engaging with Kim Jong-un and the North Korean people independently.

There have been over 30 proposed reunification plans, but none of them seem feasible. These plans merely listed what each side wanted to say, as they were merely engaged in a verbal battle with the Kim Jong-un regime. Ultimately, we must realize that reunification will only be possible when the North Korean people desire it.

Basic Framework for Reunification Centered on Theory R

Now that we have discovered the immense potential of a reunification daebak, reunification is no longer a burden but a daebak. However, this is a reality that will only be realized after reunification. The fundamental question is: how do we achieve reunification?

Realistic Reunification Plan: Voluntary Reunification

A realistic and pragmatic reunification plan can be summarized as a three-step voluntary reunification plan.

Phase 1: It is crucial for South Korean citizens to fully understand and accept the true meaning and structure of a reunification daebak, thereby forming a solid nationwide consensus on reunification. As long as South Koreans view reunification as a burden and remain divided, reunification will remain elusive.

By faithfully following the reunification daebak blueprint, we can firmly grasp the concrete fact that within ten years of reunification, the per capita income of all citizens in a unified Korea will be second only to the United States. It is essential to ensure that this truth becomes the dream and hope of all our citizens.

When all our people share this grand and exciting dream and hope for the first time in thousands of years of Korean history, and move forward together with a unified vision, reunification will become possible. We must remember the historical fact that in 2014, President Park Geun-hye's declaration that "Reunification is a daebak!" dramatically increased public support for reunification from around 53% to 82.6%, overcoming the long-standing perception that reunification was a burden.

For reunification to become possible, it is essential that all South Korean citizens first understand and believe in the reality of a reunification daebak and form a solid national consensus.

Phase 2: Once the first phase has made some progress, it is essential to gradually introduce North Korean citizens to the concept and prospects of a reunification daebak, inspiring them to share our dreams and hopes. The flow of external information should not be limited to loudspeakers along the DMZ or leaflets by balloons. There are countless ways to create these channels. We all need continuous, consistent and effective efforts, both at home and abroad.

In particular, working with conscious human rights activists in the United States to send a genuine message of the outside world to North Korean citizens will be highly effective.

However, it is crucial to ensure that North Koreans understand that the reunification daebak is not about South Korea prospering at the expense of the North or exploiting North Koreans. We must make them understand the truth that both South and North Koreans desire peace and prosperity. They must understand that this is not just empty rhetoric, unlike the countless empty promises of the Kim Il-sung dynasty over the past 80 years, such as "eating rice and meat soup in tile roof houses." For North Koreans to change their minds, they must internalize the hope and dream that a reunification daebak is not a distant future but theirs.

Phase 3: As the second phase matures, North Korean citizens must signal their readiness to abandon the cult of personality, self-reliance, and the personal monarchy of the Kim Jong-un regime, and voluntarily join a democratic, market-economy-based South Korea. This will allow our people to create a model nation united as one and embark on a path of peace and prosperity.

"Voluntary reunification" refers to a form of reunification where North Korean people, through a "Mokran Revolution" overthrowing the North Korean regime and Kim Jong-un's authoritarian communist regime, actively and voluntarily join the democratic, market-economy, and rule-of-law-based system of South Korea.

Ultimately, the specific answer to achieving reunification lies in the decision of the North Korean people to pursue voluntary reunification.

Over 30 reunification plans have been proposed since the Korean division, but none has proven to be realistic. The reason lies in their failure to consider the path of voluntary reunification and their constant attempts to compromise with the North Korean regime under the Kim family.

In the 1960s, Kim Il-sung proposed a Koryo Federation. South Korea, without a concrete reunification plan of its own, presented a three-stage reunification plan during the presidency of Roh Tae-woo. This was merely a theoretical proposal.

The three stages were inter-Korean exchange and cooperation, a confederation, and reunification. Expanding on this, President Kim Dae-jung mentioned the second stage, a confederation, to Kim Jong-il, who interpreted it as a "lower-level federation," steering the discussion towards a confederation of Korea.

The lower-level federal reunification pursued by Moon Jae-in would have been the worst-case scenario. As the history of the last century shows, countries under communism or socialist systems cannot develop.

While we could consider reunification by military force, the consequences would be unimaginable. President Kim Young-sam abandoned the idea of reunification by military force after hearing estimates of over a million casualties. Moreover, with the development of more powerful nuclear weapons, we have entered a completely different era.

When discussing reunification, people often cite the German Absorption reunification as an example. However, such a reunification is neither suitable nor feasible for us. We have a unique reunification blueprint, unlike Germany. If Germany had possessed the kind of reunification daebak framework that we have now before its reunification, the German people would not have suffered under the burden of reunification taxes for 30 years, and Germany would now be a world-leading nation.

Based on the reunification daebak framework, we must disseminate information to North Korean citizens so that they understand and accept that the benefits of reunification will be shared by both South and North Koreans. We must use every possible channel to help them learn about the realities outside of North Korea. We must inform them that if South and North Korea achieve reunification and faithfully follow the reunification daebak framework, within ten years of reunification, the per capita income of all citizens in a unified Korea will be second only to the United States. By demonstrating that they will surpass even advanced countries like Germany, the UK, France, and Japan, we must awaken North Koreans from the illusion of loyalty to Juche ideology and the Kim dynasty, and turn their hearts towards the South. This is crucial to make the North Korean people the central force driving reunification. Through this process, we can minimize sacrifices on both sides and achieve reunification while preserving North Korea's dignity. This will once again prove the truth that the will of the people is the will of heaven.

"Voluntary reunification" is theoretically grounded in the "Theory R" that I proposed in the Maeil Business Newspaper's "Shinn Chang-min's Reunification Column" in 1994.

Inside North Korea, there are actually two groups: Kim Jong-un and his followers, and the general population. Therefore, policies towards Kim Jong-un and the general population must be different.

Against Kim Jong-un, we need military force to counter his nuclear weapons. For the general population, it is essential that South Koreans and overseas Koreans provide them with information about the outside world. They must be helped to break free from generational indoctrination and make rational judgments. Ultimately, they must be determined to overthrow the Kim Jong-un communist dictatorship on their own. In fact, trying to overthrow the Kim Jong-un regime from the outside would have too many negative consequences. It is best to resolve the issue internally in North Korea.

Various Reunification Plans So Far
Since the Roh Tae-woo administration, successive governments have generally advocated a similar three-stage reunification plan,

with a "state federation" stage in the middle. However, these plans were in fact empty. They looked good but were not realistic. They may have been necessary as a form of reunification policy for external presentation in response to the Koryo Federation advocated by the North. However, we have not been able to find a realistic, fact-based reunification plan that we should pursue for the past several decades.

1. Kim Il-sung's Koryo Federation
2. Roh Tae-woo administration's Three-Stage reunification Plan (inter-Korean exchange and cooperation, confederation, reunification)
3. Three-Stage Reunification Plan (South-North reconciliation and cooperation, confederation, reunification)
4. Sunshine Policy reunification plan
5. Reunification through military force based on nuclear weapons
6. Reunification through political negotiations
7. Reunification through major powers
8. A neutral country is the answer.
9. Reunification through anti-communism
10. Peaceful reunification with an emphasis on peace
11. The path to collapse the North Korean regime through blockade and pressure
12. Kim Il-sung's 1991 New Year's address declaring, "We don't want a reunification where we are eaten up."
13. Eliminating Kim Jong-un
14. Waiting until millions starve to death and the regime collapses on its own
15. Regime Change

16. Reunification can only come through prayer.

17. Reunification can only be achieved through cultural approaches.

18. Reunification will happen when South Korea becomes advanced.

19. Giving away things for free is absolutely unacceptable.

20. Flexible reciprocity is the answer.

21. Lee Myung-bak's denuclearization, opening-up, and $3,000 policy (dismantling nuclear weapons and providing $3,000 per capita income if the North opens up)

22. Surgical Strike (targeting the vulnerable parts of North Korea, including Kim Jong-un)

23. Lower-level federal reunification (proposed by Moon Jae-in and the Democratic Party, as well as Kim Jong-il)

24. Sending leaflets by balloons and using loudspeakers towards the North

25. Utilizing North Korean defectors ("North Korean defectors are an advance reunification.")

26. The answer is reunification through the overthrow of Hell Joseon and the adoption of Kim Il-sung's Juche ideology.

Despite these various reunification plans, no realistic and effective solution has been found.

27. Recently, Kim Jong-un declared, "We are not the same people. We are different hostile states that do not need national reunification," indicating that he believes reunification under communism is difficult to achieve.

28. President Yoon Suk-yeol, "Proposal for a dialogue and consultation body between the authorities of the South

and the North, Discussion of any issue is available."
2024.8.15. Congratulatory speech

Chapter 05

Reunification Cost

I. What is the Reunification Cost?

In the practical sense of the term, the funds and costs associated with Korean reunification can be defined as follows:

- <u>Crisis management costs</u> to be used in response to emergencies such as the procurement of food, clothing, and medicine necessary to overcome the chaos immediately after reunification

- <u>Costs for unifying all systems</u> in all other fields including politics, administration, military, education, society, and culture

- This refers to <u>the sum of investment funds required to create a certain amount of real capital</u> for the purpose of reducing the income gap between the South and the North to some extent.

The costs and funds required here are all essential to completing a stable unified nation. Of course, from an economic perspective, the capital formation part is an investment concept rather than a cost. However, the background for conveniently including it in the category of reunification costs is that true reunification cannot be completed without this part being procured. In other words, it primarily means essential expenditure rather than investment in the general sense. Routine investment may not be made based on profit and loss calculations. However, the difference is that investment for the creation of physical capital in the North in reunification is not an option but a necessity that must be spent.

This investment is essential for creating physical capital in the relatively underdeveloped northern region, thereby enhancing its productive capacity. As such, it will become a part of the unified Korea's national wealth. Unlike consumption expenditures, which are depleted over time, this investment represents a long-term asset.

When dividing the various reunification funds and costs into the three types as described above, the crisis management costs for responding to emergencies and the costs for unifying various systems are relatively small and are not a major concern. Therefore, we will first analyze the investment for creating real capital in the North Korean region.

II. The Reality of Reunification Cost

1) The Scale of Reunification Cost

Through a simulation analysis of the income adjustment period between the South and the North post-reunification, it was concluded that a 10-year period is appropriate. Based on this, let's examine the estimated reunification cost.

Table 3: Summary of Estimated Reunification Cost

Income Adjustment Period Between the South & the North	Billions of USD (Constant 2013 Prices)	Ratio to South Korea's GDP
2026-2035	13,800	6.4%
2031-2040	15,662	6.4%
2036-2045	17,755	6.4%

Data Source: Shinn Chang-min, "Reunification is a Daebak," July 16, 2012

If we take appropriate steps from now on to achieve reunification, it is highly likely that reunification will be achieved by 2029. In this case, the scale of reunification cost will be approximately 7% of South Korea's GDP for the 10 years following reunification.

This 7% figure is derived by combining the costs of creating physical capital, crisis management, and unifying systems and institutions, while adjusting for overlapping areas.

2) Calculation Process and Estimation of Reunification Cost

A detailed calculation process for estimating reunification cost is provided in Appendix 3 at the end of this book. The required amount of physical capital to achieve half of the South's per capita GDP in the North 10 years after reunification was calculated, taking into account depreciation.

3) Implications of the Estimation Results

Based on the results of the above estimation and the financing methods discussed later, the following conclusions can be drawn.

First, we can afford the reunification cost.

Second, the sooner reunification occurs, the more advantageous it is in terms of both the absolute amount and the relative burden ratio to GDP at the time of reunification.

In addition to these two conclusions, we can achieve groundbreaking economic gains depending on the financing methods for reunification cost that will be discussed below.

Specifically, during the South-North income adjustment period, let's implement a "Buy Korean Products Policy" on a full scale while operating the North Korean economy separately. If we prepare the domestic and external conditions in advance, we can create a groundbreaking opportunity to achieve a 10.22% annual GDP growth rate during the 10-year South-North income adjustment period (from South Korea's perspective alone).

Chapter 06

Securing Other Direct Reunification Costs Financing

1) Issuance of Overseas Loans and Overseas Bonds

It is desirable to obtain long-term low-interest loans from international financial institutions such as the IBRD, ADB, and AIIB for 1% of the GDP required for reunification cost. These international financial institutions support the economic development of developing countries. It is crucial to pursue the introduction of loans while emphasizing the fact that the northern region was extremely underdeveloped in the world until just before reunification and the international peace and stability that reunification will bring. At the same time, efforts should be made to reflect a favorable position in loan introduction terms based on the fact that the unified Korea's repayment capacity is sufficient.

If funding through foreign loans falls short of the 1% GDP target, it will be necessary to have a supplementary measure of issuing foreign bonds. In other words, it is appropriate to introduce a total of 1% of funds from overseas. If the overseas procurement is insufficient, it can lead to an overload of domestic direct procurement.

2) Government Bonds and Taxes

Of the total reunification cost, 2% from reduced military spending, 1% from overseas low-interest loans, and the remaining 4% of

GDP must be directly procured by South Korean citizens. It is considered appropriate to solve the 2% of GDP each year for the 10-year period of South-North income adjustment through taxes and the issuance of reunification bonds. Originally, taxes were expected to be smaller, but since the national debt suddenly exceeded 1,000 trillion won from 600 trillion won due to the Moon Jae-in's chaos, it is inevitable to adjust taxes from 1% to 2%. Government bonds represent 2% of income and have the meaning of intergenerational sharing of reunification cost. This is because the benefits and benefits obtained from reunification will continue to be enjoyed by all members of society over generations after reunification.

Germany did not have such a comprehensive pre-planning framework, so they had to bear the heavy burden of a 7.5% reunification tax from 1991 to 1998 and a 5.5% reunification tax from 1999 to 2020.

However, it is important to note that it is undesirable to prepare and stockpile reunification taxes or government bonds in advance, regardless of the circumstances. It is sufficient to create them as needed when they are needed. We must prevent unnecessary leakage from the economic flow due to the collection of reunification taxes, which would otherwise cause the economy to shrink. I hope there is no misunderstanding among the public about this.

There have also been discussions about converting defense taxes into reunification taxes, but this is undesirable as it simply repackages an idea from the past confrontational situation. There have also been discussions about doing it in the form of a value-added tax, but this imposes the same burden on the rich and the poor. As a result, it becomes a regressive tax, placing a greater burden on the economically disadvantaged, which is inappropriate.

On the other hand, there have been opinions to collect funds through the South-North Cooperation Fund, and the concept of a "Reunification Jar" has also circulated. However, this form of fundraising is bound to have its limitations. Moreover, just as reunification taxes should not be stockpiled and used when needed, this is also not an appropriate method.

Chapter 07

Reunification Benefits

To grasp the benefits gained from reunification in more detail, we will divide them into the following three periods:

1. Benefits from the elimination of division costs immediately after reunification.
2. Vast economic benefits that will appear during the 10-year period of South-North income adjustment after reunification.
3. Benefits and prosperity that will continue to appear after 10 years of reunification.

1) Benefits From the Elimination of Division Cost

In a divided state, division cost that cannot be avoided inevitably occur. Since the very cause of these division cost disappears with reunification, there is a benefit equal to the amount that no longer needs to be paid for division cost. In other words, it means the difference from the negative magnitude of the division cost returning to zero, which was the original point.

Division cost include all opportunity costs caused by division, such as loss of life, suffering of separated families, all inconveniences, anxiety, disadvantages, losses, excessive defense spending, waste of manpower, and risks.

The specific economic benefits of this are as follows:

• During the income adjustment period, military spending can be reduced and replaced with an annual production of general consumer goods and capital goods equivalent to 2% of GDP, and a significant increase in production can be obtained after that period due to the multiplier effect.

• By reducing the South's military manpower, it is possible to increase production by an average of 2.4% of GDP annually over the 10-year adjustment period, and even after that period, a significant increase in production can be obtained, although to a lesser extent.

• Individuals will regain opportunities that were lost due to the mandatory military service under the divided state, allowing them to maximize their human capital during their youth.

• As social overhead capital facilities are gradually expanded in the northern region, the underground resources of the northern region, which have not been fully utilized until now, will demonstrate their true value.

• Due to the division, South Korea has been cut off from the continental land route, leading to higher transportation costs and other logistics costs. Additionally, routes passing through the airspace of the northern region from South Korea have been blocked, requiring detours. This has resulted in unnecessary additional costs, including fuel, and psychological distance. By reunification, these disadvantages and waste will disappear.

• With the opening of a continental route, it will be possible to directly import low-cost natural gas from Russia through a pipeline, greatly contributing to energy procurement. This will lead to lower production costs and improved international competitiveness.

• The market will expand through the reunification of the South and the North, and we will be able to gain benefits from economies of scale.

• Complementary advantages in various science and technologies can be utilized. If the North has relatively strong areas in basic sciences, these can be combined with the South's market-related know-how to create synergy effects.

• For South Korean residents, the reason why the cost of visiting Mount Kumgang was extremely high was that they had to pay additional costs beyond the actual costs due to the division. The extra money paid in cash is also a type of cost associated with division. The benefit of eliminating these unnecessary costs will arise.

• Mount Kumgang can be visited by paying explicit costs. However, other scenic spots located in the northern region, such as Mount Baekdu and Mount Myohyang, could not be visited. The satisfaction and benefits that can be obtained from these tourist resources can be regained with reunification.

• Many parts of the beautiful mountains and rivers of South and North Korea, which have been distorted by barbed wire due to division, will return to their original natural state. Our lives will become more comfortable within this environment, and excellent tourist resources will regain their original form.

• The names and political slogans of the former monarch Kims, which were deeply engraved on the beautiful rocks of the mountains, will be removed, restoring the environment.

• Foreign investors can invest directly without worries as the risk of war or armed conflict is eliminated. This creates jobs domestically and increases GDP.

• The unified country benefits from reduced interest burdens in the international financial market due to the risk premium associated with the divided situation.

• The Korea discount phenomenon disappears. The stock market receives a proper valuation.

The non-economic benefits are as follows:

• Separated families can heal their wounds and overcome the pain of division.

• The risk of large and small armed conflicts between the South and the North, which could occur at any time, is eliminated. This removes the cause of the unfortunate loss of life.

• People can live in true peace, freed from the tension inherent in everyday life due to the military confrontation between the South and the North.

• For North Korean residents, they will enter the world of free human beings from a state where human rights were nothing more than a luxurious illusion.

• People can be free from unnecessary restrictions in their daily lives that have often appeared due to national defense and security issues in the past.

• The country will escape from the weak national status due to the division and finally acquire the appearance of a strong nation, and citizens will gain the status befitting citizens of a proud nation overseas.

2) 10-Year Period Immediately After Reunification

In order to reduce the income gap between the South and the North immediately after reunification, a huge amount of funds equivalent to about 7% of the South's GDP at that time will be invested in the northern region every year, resulting in a remarkable growth in the North's production capacity. During this process, the per capita income of the North will catch up to half of that of the South. Centered on the huge economic benefits generated in the southern region due to the production and supply of most physical capital from the southern region, the South will also achieve a dazzling economic growth of 10.22% annually for 10 years after reunification, based on the "effective demand" formed by financing reunification costs. This alone is a real daebak.

Benefits, conveniences, and types of profits are as follows:

• In the process of forming physical capital for North Korean production, let's go with the "Buy Korean Product" policy, where most of the capital goods, equivalent to 7% of South Korea's GDP each year for 10 years, can be produced and supplied by the South. The resulting production effects, multiplier effects, and industrial linkage effects will have a tremendous ripple effect, and our economy will achieve a second dazzling economic leap, surpassing the economic leap of President Park Chung-hee's era, with an annual economic growth rate of 10.22%.

South
Annual economic growth of 10.22%:
1. Buy Korean Products Policy: GDP 5.6%
2. Trend growth: 2.7%
3. Productivity increase due to the abolition of military service: 1.92%
* Others (North Korea's abundant underground resources, passage to the continent, economies of scale, etc., additional portions exist)
Total 10.22%

North
10 years after reunification,
More than half of South Korea's per capita income of US$ 83,094 achieved.
Per capita income in North Korea under Kim Jong-un increased by more than 40 times.

• With the reunification and unrestricted connection of railways, roads, ports, routes, and communications to the continent, a unified Korea, located in the geographical environment at the center of the continent and the ocean, can directly advance to both the continent and the ocean. It will gain opportunities to reduce logistics costs and transportation costs and expand overseas markets. As a result, a unified Korea can emerge as a central hub in the East Asian region in various fields such as logistics and finance. Historically, due to its location between the continent and the ocean, Korea has suffered greatly from many disadvantages, but now this has turned into a favorable advantage, leading to a time of turning misfortune into good fortune by expanding in both directions, the continent and the ocean.

• Due to the demand for manpower for the production of capital goods and for the process of unifying various systems under the Buy Korean Products policy, a situation of manpower shortage appears, unemployment disappears, and a state of job abundance is created.

• The relatively abundant underground resources of the North, which had little value due to the poor social overhead capital facilities of the North in a divided state, can now demonstrate their true value.

• Secure low-cost energy through the installation of a direct natural gas pipeline from Russia.

• Gain benefits from economies of scale as the economy expands.

• After reunification, North Korean residents, who will become citizens of a unified Korea, will account for one-third of the total population. They will enjoy the benefits and status of becoming citizens of a powerful nation at the forefront of the world, leaping from a subhuman, miserable life to a level that surpasses even that of ordinary advanced countries.

• With reunification, the concept of land public ownership, where ownership and usage rights are separated, will be introduced starting from the northern region and expanded nationwide. By getting rid of the incurable disease of real estate speculation and eliminating one of the chronic causes of market failure, we will have a framework for an efficient market economy. As a result, we will achieve a rational and equitable income distribution framework along with economic development. This will make our country a model among market economy countries.

3) 10 Years After Reunification

After achieving reunification and going through a period of South-North income adjustment, we will gain many tangible and intangible benefits as we transition from a divided nation to a truly unified nation. In other words, we will enjoy a happy life in peace, which is possible thanks to a stable national security foundation, not only during the South-North income adjustment period but also after the completion of reunification, as well as benefits, profits, and the creation of profits, economies of scale, increases in production factors such as population, territory, and underground resources, and technological advancements. In all areas, convenience, ease, and economic growth and development at the national level, capital accumulation, strengthening of national power, and improvement of international competitiveness will follow. In short, we will usher in an era of prosperity in peace.

Specifically, the following benefits, conveniences, and profits can be seen:

• Even after the income adjustment period ends, the northern region will continue to have a substantial demand for capital goods, following the trend of capital accumulation. This will continue to drive the South Korean economy.

• By realizing the complementarity of production resources between the South and the North, production can be increased.

• As the production and consumption levels of the northern region begin to rise due to the formation of capital in it, the number of areas where economies of scale can be achieved will increase, based on the expanded market size due to reunification. We can produce larger quantities at relatively lower prices. As a result, international competitiveness will also increase.

• In the northern region, the situation of late development can be turned into an opportunity to directly enter an advanced economic structure by drawing on a blank slate, and through this connection, harmonious and desirable economic belts and lifestyles can be formed in various regions across the country.

• In the agricultural sector, if we introduce a circular organic farming system in the northern regions like Hwanghae Province and Pyongan Province, where the soil has not been contaminated by chemical fertilizers, producers can create high added value. People living in densely populated areas will benefit greatly from improved diets and health by consuming high-quality, uncontaminated agricultural products.

• While maintaining the economic growth trend of the southern region, we will form a larger economic scale through increased production in the northern region. Based on this, we will acquire the appearance of a truly prosperous country with a proper territory and a significant population.

• After reunification, as the South and North regions enter a mixed stage after economic separation management, the country will acquire the appearance of a truly unified nation along with the standardization of systems in various fields that will be achieved simultaneously during the same period.

• A considerable period after reunification, a unified Korea will become a powerful nation that no one in the Northeast Asian region can easily ignore. It will also have the status of a proud nation in terms of international diplomacy.

• Unified Korea will subsequently have a great status as a truly independent nation and the glory of national self-esteem for generations to come. Reunification is, in fact, a way to complete the bloody independence movement of our ancestors.

If we add various other benefits and conveniences from reunification that cannot be listed one by one, the benefits, conveniences, and profits gained from reunification will naturally show a much larger gap than the reunification cost.

Chapter 08

Two Important Issues of Real and Direct Concern to the South Korean People Regarding Reunification

Recently, we have come to focus on the following two important issues in a realistic manner:

I. Unification Tax

First of all, I want to make it clear that there is no need to fear the unification tax associated with the reunification cost. A unification tax in the form of a direct payment by citizens is possible at 2% of individual income in the South. Originally, this unification tax was to be at the 1% level, but after the Moon Jae-in administration, the national debt jumped from 600 trillion won to over 1,000 trillion won, resulting in the aftermath. However, it will all be settled with a 2% tax on total individual income for a fixed period of 10 years after reunification. Other unification cost will be covered by other methods, and there will be no more direct taxes to be directly borne in relation to reunification. During that period, the South Korean economy is preparing to greet us with a phenomenal economic growth rate of 10.22%.

II. Jobs

South Korea is currently suffering from high unemployment rates, especially among young people. If, in addition to this, cheap labor from North Korea suddenly floods in, we may be wondering what we should do. However, this is a completely misplaced worry that comes from a failure to properly understand the reality.

First of all, it is essential to manage the South and North regions separately in terms of economics for 10 years after reunification. And when reunification occurs, jobs will actually overflow. In the process of raising North Korea's income for 10 years after reunification, South Korea's production must increase significantly due to the production of physical capital goods required for the North. In addition, there will be a high demand for manpower from the South in the process of unifying various systems. As a result, unemployment will disappear, and we will reach a situation that is even higher than full employment.

Also, even before reunification, if we decide to gradually start building North Korea's social infrastructure, we can approach the North Korean people and activate the domestic economy in South Korea by producing and supplying all the necessary hardware to the North. So how can we actually achieve the enormous results of reunification? The answer can be found by comprehensively analyzing the reunification costs, reunification funds, and reunification benefits together.

Chapter 09

Is There Another Reunification Daebak Other Than the Contents of This Book?

There is no other. Without the fundamental conditions and four crucial conditions for reunification daebak, the concept of reunification daebak cannot exist.

When the term "reunification daebak" emerged, many people showed interest. However, nowhere else on earth can provide a clear path to reunification daebak.

A paper published by the Reunification Preparatory Committee states that if North Korea adopts a market economy system, it will achieve a large harvest with an annual economic growth rate of 4% by 2050. What is the meaning of such a prediction based on this premise? Can we simply ignore the fact that North Korea is a group that cannot adopt a market economy system because maintaining the regime is its top priority?

Meanwhile, the Financial Services Commission has stated that no reunification tax is needed. They envision that by raising funds through the financial sector and private investment, North Korea's per capita income can be raised to $10,000 within 20 years of reunification. However, when comparing the same period, the South is expected to reach $50,000 through trend growth alone.

Can a society remain stable within a unified nation where the average income gap between regions is 5 to 1?

Also, when it was announced that South Korea's per capita

GDP would become the second highest in the world 10 years after reunification under the reunification daebak framework, the reaction was, "Oh, didn't Goldman Sachs say something like that?" Goldman Sachs made a vague prediction several years ago, looking 40 years into the future, based on North Korea's underground resources and excellent workforce. Is there a significance of that?

A famous lecturer receives enthusiastic applause by saying that we will achieve reunification daebak and become the world's number one in 50 years. What is the meaning of economic forecasts that look half a century ahead without any solid basis?

Some people think of Jim Rogers when they hear about reunification daebak. He simply made a remark based on the abundant underground resources and excellent workforce of North Korea from the perspective of a foreign investor. While individual investors may benefit to some extent from that, reunification daebak at the national level does not occur.

All of these are vastly different from the reunification daebak framework of this book, which analyzes the situation based on realistic effective demand within a comprehensive macro-economic framework.

Chapter 10

South-South Conflict – The Right and The Left

Traditionally, the South-South conflict has been approached as an issue between conservatism and progressivism. However, after the Moon Jae-in administration, this perspective has become less useful.

It is now more practical to classify people as right-wing or left-wing.

Let's first clearly distinguish the right-wing and then classify all other cases as left-wing for convenience.

The right-wing is based on liberal democracy, market economy, and the rule of law. For convenience, we will temporarily classify all other positions as left-wing.

In the reality of South Korea, for the sake of convenience, let's classify all ideologies that are not right-wing, such as Kim Il-sung's Juche ideology, the Koryo Federation, or a lower-stage federation, the Chinese Communist Party system, the Russian authoritarian regime, communism, socialist communism, social democracy, South Korean Socialist Workers' League, socialism, and Nordic-style socialism, as left-wing.

This is because liberal democracy, market economy, and the rule of law are essential underlying conditions for the completion of reunification daebak, so we can conveniently define them as right-wing and classify other positions as a mixed left-wing for the time being.

After achieving reunification, during the 10-year period from the following fiscal year to complete reunification daebak, if we become the second-highest per capita income country in the world, right after the United States, we may subsequently incorporate some aspects of socialism while realizing the world of Hongik Ingan.

However, before that, we must keep in mind that if the leftist position is emphasized, it will be easy to make the completion of a unified world impossible.

Chapter 11

Preparation of a Master Plan for Development of North Korea After Reunification

Above all, it is crucial to develop a detailed master plan for the development of the North Korean region. Only by doing so can we start investing in North Korean infrastructure before formal reunification or build the necessary social infrastructure in the northern region after reunification and foster harmonious development and organic relationships across the entire country by following this guideline.

If we simply allow the northern region to be haphazardly developed according to the interests of individual companies or individuals, it will result in a disastrous and irreversible situation.

The master plan for the development of the northern region should create a future-oriented growth blueprint that fully considers the specific characteristics of each region, its regional background of natural resources such as underground resources, and the complexity and feasibility of technology levels.

Chapter 12

Words to Our Fellow North Koreans

1. When my book "Reunification is a Daebak" was published in 2012, our compatriots in the North immediately criticized, saying, "Are all South Koreans economic animals? Reunification is a national aspiration, not a daebak." I believe they thought that reunification daebak was a scheme for the South to benefit by exploiting the North. This is probably because they are well aware that western investors are eyeing North Korea's abundant resources and cheap labor. However, reunification daebak is the best scenario where both the South and the North join forces and win together. It's not a shallow intention of one side trying to exploit the other. Foreigners can come to North Korea, take advantage of it, and leave. Our goal is not to exploit each other but to work hard together and live well together. I hope there is no misunderstanding about it.

In fact, the phrase "utilization of abundant underground resources or cheap labor" does not even appear in the initial part of the North Korean economic development plan. That is something that can be discussed when the economy grows enough to utilize underground resources, and it is of no help in the early stages of reunification.

And while foreign capitalists can make profits by using cheap labor, we, as Koreans, are not people who use or go anywhere, are we?

2. Our compatriots in the North should not be too greedy right after reunification but should steadily and systematically build up step by step. For 10 years after reunification, North Korean residents should actively open the path to economic development in order to rapidly increase production and income, in response to the cooperation of the South.

3. If people had to do bad things in the past to survive in the given North Korean system, it may be different from crimes in a normal society. Therefore, it may not be reasonable to deal with past actions under the previous regime solely through punishment after reunification. However, we should remember to keep records and avoid committing any more harsh and reckless acts against our fellow Koreans until reunification.

4. From now on, the various aspects of the world of reunification daebak will continue to be revealed in various forms. There is no need to rush, but we should gradually become familiar with it and when we all feel that the time is ripe, I hope that all compatriots in the North will rise up together, risking their lives, and raise the torch of the Mokran Revolution that will overthrow the communist regime of Kim Jong-un that exploits the people.

5. Some people in South Korea may have bad habits and want to quickly enter the North Korean region to speculate on real estate and I hope they will give up that idea from the beginning. Real estate speculation in the North is a path to ruin for both the South and the North. The government should fundamentally prevent

such speculative activities from the beginning and impose severe penalties that cannot be appealed for violations. North Korean residents should also know that if they participate in this, they will all perish together.

> Reunification is our wish, our long-cherished desire.
> Now is the time to create reunification with our own hands.
> We must make it done with our own hands.
> No one else but us can bring reunification for us and on our behalf.
> Reunification cannot be achieved through guns or nuclear weapons, nor through political negotiations between those in power.
> Blocking pressure from outside has its limits.

When over 75 million people in both South and North Korea understand, believe, and work together towards the hope of "Reunification is a daebak," only then can reunification be achieved.

Through reunification, the people of North and South Korea can all live prosperous lives in peace, live as human beings with dignity, and pass on a proud and great unified country to our future generations.

Reunification is truly a daebak. A daebak means something incredibly good. Reunification is a real daebak for all of South Koreans, North Koreans, and overseas Koreans.

For example, if the per capita income of South Koreans is around $34,000 at the time of reunification (currently, North Korea's per capita income is slightly above $1,000), the average per capita income of North Korean people will exceed $40,000 within 10 years. That's almost 40 times the current level.

It's truly a daebak! The per capita income of North Korea will be much higher than that of South Korea at the time of reunification. South and North Koreans will then live completely freely, as human beings with dignity. We will rise to a level that is not inferior to any advanced country in the world. The promise of "rice with meat soup" made by Chairman Kim Il-sung for three generations was just a playful joke. More importantly, we will no longer need to look up to superiors or anyone else.

When we say reunification is a daebak, some South Koreans might suspect that, like the foreign investor Jim Rogers, South Koreans have ulterior motives to exploit the cheap labor and abundant resources of the North Korean people. But that's absolutely not the case.

After reunification, South Korea will achieve tremendous economic growth based on the effective demand generated from producing and providing all the physical capital needed for North Korea's economic development.

In the North, they will receive this physical capital and work hard to achieve remarkable economic development based on their performance. It's not a situation where one side takes from the other. We will cooperate with each other and become completely one.

For the next 10 years after reunification, both the South and the North will achieve remarkable economic development separately. The South has already prepared separate means to secure the necessary funds for this. Please don't worry and work together according to the plans set up by the South. We have new hopes and dreams that fill our hearts. We must never give up or let go of hope. I hope we will all continue to work together until the day we become the ultimate winners.

Finally, I have one more thing to add. The people living in the North are all our people, our fellow Koreans. They are all our blood relatives. In the past, there were many mistakes that had to be made under the ideology and thought. We must now cover this all up. Retaliation only begets retaliation, and an enemy only begets an enemy. We must end everything here. We should open a way for the Kim family to go into exile, and everyone else should be able to live well together without having to flee abroad. However, we must record the past mistakes so that they can serve as a lesson for future generations. I emphasize again that *we should forgive but not forget.*

We must all follow this path and enter the path of coexistence while minimizing the aftereffects of reunification. In South Korea, a repository for records related to North Korean human rights has already been established. The Ministry of Unification collects data and transfers it to the Ministry of Justice for preservation. Please keep this in mind and reduce any excessive mistreatment of each other within North Korea from now on. This will make it much easier for us to be at ease with each other after reunification.

There are some crucial points that our North Korean compatriots must be aware of in advance to avoid confusion.

Even after reunification, everyone can freely travel throughout the unified Korea without needing anyone's permission. However, for the 10-year period of achieving reunification daebak, you will continue to have jobs in the northern region. And during that period, the formation of labor unions will not be allowed. All of this is to achieve the goal of reunification daebak in the shortest time possible with the least cost. It is not intended to discriminate against North Korean residents. The unified government will provide jobs for all North Korean residents. You don't have to wander around looking for jobs in unfamiliar areas.

Of course, the government will provide essential goods for free for a while before you get paid. You don't have to worry or look at anyone. You don't have to bribe anyone. The unified government will provide everything you need for as long as necessary.

After the 10-year period of achieving reunification daebak, all restrictions will be lifted, and everyone will have complete freedom.

To create such a world of reunification daebak, reunification must first be achieved. This is something that North Korean compatriots must create themselves. Kim Jong-un will never voluntarily give up his throne. If we try to solve it through war, no one can predict how many millions or even tens of millions of people will die. The best way is to induce Kim Jong-un to go into exile. If he refuses until the end, there will be no choice but to eliminate him. There is no need for 25 million people to continue to live as slaves and starve while one person plays the role of king. For the past 80 years, have the promises of tile roof houses, beef, and rice been kept? Don't believe in such empty promises anymore. Now, let's all go out together to create a new world. It's a world of K-dream that the world will envy. When the time is ripe, please gather your strength and take action!

Chapter 13

The Facts

1. North Korea Nuclear Issue

The South Korean government can propose to the North Korean regime to stop playing games with nuclear weapons and to give them up now.

But can we force the North Korean regime to surrender through international pressure or blockade? Is that really the case?

In a situation where the North Korean regime has only nuclear weapons to rely on, how can we expect it to give up its nuclear weapons for any price based on rational judgment? What can guarantee the security of the North Korean regime? By signing a treaty? By an international agreement between countries? Considering that the North Korean regime unilaterally declared the armistice agreement no longer valid, can we believe that it will firmly believe the treaties of other countries?

It seems that Kim Jong-un is destined to end up rolling around with nuclear weapons and missiles.

2. Peaceful Coexistence

Those who emphasize the 6.15 Declaration and the 10.4 Declaration often focus on "peace" in peaceful reunification. However, we need to face the harsh reality that peaceful coexistence does not necessarily lead to reunification even after 100 years.

Basically, peace does not come just by shouting for it. If you truly want peace, you must have strength. Choosing peace is something that can be discussed only after you have gained strength.

Moreover, those who consider a peace treaty should also think about the next step. If a peace treaty is concluded as the North Korean regime wants, the next thing that will follow is the "withdrawal of US troops." Because the presence of US troops does not make sense after a peace treaty is concluded.

From the perspective of a unified Korea, it is absolutely necessary for US troops to remain stationed at least for the first 10 years of reunification, for the sake of stabilizing the unified nation, reducing cost, and defending the territory. It is one of the essential and important factors for the completion of reunification daebak. Therefore, the continued presence of US troops is not a unilateral sacrifice by the United States. This is because the United States desperately needs a presence in Korea to check China. The United States is certainly aware that the US military presence in Korea is actually economical for the United States. The United States must also internally recognize that the US presence in Korea is not a unilateral sacrifice by the United States for Korea.

During the Moon Jae-in administration, Moon Jae-in traveled around the world, persuading for a peace treaty. It seemed as if he was treating Kim Jong-un as the head of his suzerain state and speaking on his behalf. It was just embarrassing how foreign countries would have viewed him for such a ridiculous act.

3. Anti-communism and Security

In the context of the division of the Korean Peninsula, anti-communism and security are essential. If this collapses, the freedom and democracy and market economy that we seek will disappear without a trace. However, many people seem to have lost sight of their ultimate goal while struggling with anti-communism and security. That should not be. It is a big mistake to have a vague expectation that reunification will come someday if we do well in anti-communism and security. We must continue our tireless efforts to go beyond anti-communism and security and win over the hearts of North Korean people, ultimately leading to reunification.

Our goal is reunification, not permanent division. With permanent division, our nation will eventually collapse and perish.

4. Absorption Reunification Leads to Perishing?

That's wrong. Of course, reunification without preparation will not succeed. In fact, if we absorb North Korea in the German style, we will fail. We cannot even handle that kind of reunification. But we have our own successful path. We have already prepared our own unique framework, which Germany could never dream of. It is the reunification daebak achievement framework.

If the North Korean regime collapses at any time, we can successfully lead reunification daebak if we are well prepared in the South according to the contents of the reunification daebak framework. The problem is that reunification will not be easy regardless of the route taken, but once reunification is achieved, complete integration after South Korea-led economic construction will be the most efficient, least wasteful, and most desirable. On the contrary, absorption reunification is the most desirable if it is possible. What is important is to be thoroughly prepared for reunification daebak in case of such an event.

5. Sudden Reunification Will Lead to Failure.

No, that's not true. Regardless of when reunification occurs, if all our people are aware of what to do and how to do it at the time of reunification and are familiar with the four crucial conditions for reunification daebak mentioned above, we can proceed directly to daebak. Therefore, it is important for our people to have a realistic and common understanding of reunification daebak. As soon as reunification occurs in any situation, let's enter the four prepared frameworks. Then we can create successful reunification daebak.

There is also a view that it will be difficult to separate the South and the North for 10 years due to sudden reunification, but this is also the same. There is always a way for those who seek it. It all depends on whether we all keep in mind the four crucial conditions and our mental preparedness. Moreover, since the draft of Reunification Daebak Special Act has been presented above, we can follow the smooth path to successful reunification.

6) China And Other Surrounding Powers

"Reunification depends on the interests of surrounding countries such as China. It is not something that can be done by our own strength."

If we are intimidated from the beginning like this, reunification cannot be achieved.

In the case of Germany, reunification was achieved even when all four surrounding powers openly opposed reunification. In our case, at least, there is no outward opposition, right?

China would not be happy about Korea-led reunification either, but China has recently been changing to a more pragmatic approach in terms of practicality. Ultimately, it is up to us, the main actors. If we give up from the beginning, nothing will happen. However, we need to subtly remind China at every opportunity that the US military will never move north and station itself before or after reunification, conscious of China.

Japan may easily think that it is easier to deal with the Korean Peninsula if it remains divided. However, if we broaden our perspective to a global perspective, if the Korean Peninsula is unified and wisely establishes itself as a clearly stable free democratic country, the benefits of peaceful exchanges between Korea and Japan will be much greater.

7) The Issue of Defectors

The most important thing for us to have a proper attitude toward defectors is to cooperate so that they can settle down well, adapt to this society, and live well. It is not good to think about directly utilizing them for reunification. It is also not desirable to have excessive expectations of them. It is most important that their families and relatives in the North know that they have settled down and are living well.

Of course, there are various roles that only they can play after reunification. However, there is no need to exaggerate this in advance.

8) The Truth and Falsehood of Kim Jong-un's Parallel Nuclear and Economic Development Policy

Kim Jong-un's true intention is that possessing nuclear weapons is absolutely necessary to protect his regime. He says that only then will economic development be possible.

On the other hand, the Western world believes that North Korea cannot protect its regime with nuclear weapons alone and must reform and open.

However, both above views are wrong.

Let's assume that Kim Jong-un's possession of nuclear weapons is recognized, and that economic development can be built on that basis. Even so, the political and economic system that North Korea has cannot avoid poverty and cannot feed its people. Even if it tries to reform and open in its own way with that system, it will not be able to make even a few steps forward. The income gap between the South and the North will only widen further, and eventually the North Korean regime will not be able to find a reason for its existence.

On the other hand, the Western world's perspective is wrong because they are turning a blind eye to the fact that North Korea cannot reform and open. They are just talking nonsense because the North's possession of nuclear weapons is inconvenient.

So, what is the fate of the North? As a result, the only answer that can come out is the demise of the North Korean regime sooner or later. Making absurd and unreasonable demands that go against the grain will not last long.

9) Human Rights Issues

It is heartbreaking to see our fellow North Koreans living under oppression.

It is natural to bring up human rights issues for them. However, no matter how loudly we shout about the improvement of human rights, the reality of North Korea is that nothing will change.

Even if the human rights movement is important, it is not a problem that will be solved until reunification is realized. It is not because our laws are lacking. It is not because international cooperation is lacking. It is because there is no fundamental solution without reunification. From the perspective of the North Korean regime, human rights are merely a secondary or tertiary issue in terms of maintaining the regime.

From the perspective of the US government, there is not much that can be done for the North Korean people. However, US civic groups can play a very important role. If we cooperate with Korean civic groups and make efforts to inform the North Korean people of the reality of the outside world of North Korea through various channels, the ripple effect could be remarkable. This could act as a new source of vitality for the North Korean people who are discouraged, resigned, and unable to find a breakthrough, and it could be an effective way to dream and hope for achieving reunification daebak and open a path directly to reunification, ultimately leading to the demise of the North Korean regime.

It is necessary to emphasize once again the realistic importance of the North Korean human rights movement achieved through Korea-US cooperation.

10) Korea-US Relations

During the process of Korea being liberated from Japan, becoming independent, and establishing a government, and during the difficulties of the Korean War, the US responded to President Rhee Syngman's intentions and efforts by providing indescribable help to Korea and forming a strong blood alliance.

The future of Korea cannot be imagined without the strong blood alliance between Korea and the US.

However, the strong blood alliance between Korea and the US is not only important to Korea but is also an essential element of the US's East Asian strategic national interest.

The problem is that Korea is becoming communist(?) without realizing it. Only by coming to its senses can we convey the essential message for improving the US-ROK relationship that is going wrong.

① Above all, we must liquidate the Moon Jae-in era and return to liberal democracy, market economy, and rule of law.

The Moon Jae-in government had in fact derailed all three.

We do not want communism, communist socialism, or any form of socialism. Above all, without liberal democracy, the economy cannot grow in earnest.

② The United States supported Korea's independence, saved Korea from communism during the Korean War, and became its blood ally. Now Korea needs America's help again.

Now it must escape Kim Jong-un's nuclear weapons threats.

It is impossible without America's help.

The Moon Jae-in government in Korea has been acting ambiguously between the United States and China.

Anti-Americanism was just a slogan for Moon Jae-in's faction.

Most of the people are grateful to the United States.

③ Presidents G.W. Bush and Obama were more interested in unifying the entire Korean Peninsula into a free democratic nation than in protecting Korea and the U.S. forces stationed in South Korea.

That is the right path for both the United States and Korea.

From the U.S.'s perspective, it is especially advantageous for the confrontation between communist forces in the East Asian region if the Korean Peninsula becomes a free democratic unified Korea.

④ If Korea achieves free democratic reunification, even if the United States does not directly intervene in the economy of the North, the unified Korea will be able to grow well together with the South and the North. For example, there is no need for the United States to work hard to increase income in the North as much as Vietnam.

A tremendous "reunification daebak framework" has been prepared in Korea after reunification ("Daebak" Reunification: Tremendous <u>Prosperity in Peace</u>)

⑤ On the path to Korean reunification, the most urgent task is to separate the North Korean people from the North Korean regime. To do this, it would be effective to clearly raise the issue of human rights, as in the Biden policy. However, the Moon Jae-in government has been blocking the inflow of external information into the North by law. Moon Jae-in only thought about the North Korean regime and reunification under a federal system, and did not have any consideration for free democratic reunification or the North Korean people.

⑥ Now, as the Korea-US generals association, America Korea United Society (AKUS) becoming more active in the United States, we greatly expect that AKUS, which is showing significant interest in the human rights issue of the North Korean people on the Korean Peninsula, will continue to play a substantial and powerful role.

⑦ Korea had high expectations for President Trump, but there was a problem with the direction. He said that if North Korea gives up its nuclear weapons, he will make them live well like Vietnam. We do not want the North Korean economy to fall to the level of Vietnam, which is only 1/12th of the South Korean economy, while the South and the North are divided.

South Korea has already established a structure for completing a reunification daebak, in which the average income per capita in the South and the North will rise to the second place in the world after the United States 10 years after reunification.

In the process of the United States making North Korea as prosperous as Vietnam, North Korea will also escape starvation, and the United States may also benefit to some extent from the results of its investment in North Korea. However, compared to the strong economic power of the unified Korea, which will make the average income per capita of the entire population rise to the second place after the United States, and the unified Korea will play a solid and important role in the US-China confrontation, the benefit is only like a very small investment benefit. If the United States leads Korea to reunification and makes it a cutting-edge base for the US through rapid growth, it will gain an ally on the Korean Peninsula that is much more powerful and effective than Japan.

11) Expanding Access to External Information for North Korean Residents: *President Yoon Suk-yeol's Celebration Speech on August 15, 2024*

In President Yoon Suk-yeol's Celebration Speech on August 15, 2024, he stated that we must pursue tasks that will encourage and change North Korean residents so that they strongly desire free reunification. This means that we must expand access to information so that North Korean residents can access external information through various channels.

I believe that this is the beginning of our progress toward reunification.

However, if we stop here, it will be nothing more than empty words. Therefore, we hope that at this point, we can connect what President Yoon preached with the existing blueprint for a reunification daebak and sublimate it into a shining achievement that will be sublimated into an effective and realistic reunification policy. It should not be something that started with words and ended with words.

Above all, we must ensure that North Korean people fully understand the reality of the reunification daebak, so that the reunification daebak becomes their own hopeful and certain future, a future that they all dream of.

❊ *Appendix 3: Calculation Process for Each Step of Calculating Reunification Required Funds*

A significant portion of the costs associated with successfully achieving reunification lies in the investment required to establish physical capital in the northern region. This investment, rather than being a consumable expense, is intended to accumulate national wealth and stimulate production growth. There is no need for unnecessary burden or resistance.

The required annual investment amount for capital formation can be calculated through the following steps based on the Harrod-Domar growth model:

① First, the GDP gap between the South and North must be estimated for the target year when income adjustment between the divided regions is complete. This calculation assumes that the South and North economies would follow their own independent growth paths, even without reunification. This implies that the southern economy will not be hindered or sacrificed to assist the North after reunification, and thus, there is no reason for South Koreans to have a sense of unnecessary paranoid

② By multiplying the estimated population of the North in the target year by the calculated GDP gap, we can determine the total output required to completely bridge the gap. To achieve this level of annual output, assuming a capital-output ratio of 2.2, a physical capital stock equal to twice this amount is necessary.

③ However, as a practical compromise, if we aim to unify the South and North economies into a single economic bloc when the northern income level reaches half that of the South, then only half of the required capital would be needed.

④ Considering the usable portion of land and buildings, as well as exploitable mineral resources in the North, let's assume that the existing physical capital in the northern region is approximately 1/6 of the required capital calculated above. Therefore, by multiplying the previously calculated required capital by 5/6, we obtain the actual amount of physical capital that needs to be created in the North.

⑤ To achieve the target level of capital formation by the target year, annual investment is calculated to increase at the same rate as the expected GDP growth rate of the South for the convenience of fundraising. Considering that a certain portion of the total investment is depreciated each year, the investment amount that should be invested at the beginning of the income adjustment period between the South and North is calculated as follows:

$$X_1 = \frac{\text{Total amount of real capital to be raised by the target year } j}{\sum_{i=1}^{j} (\text{Southern GDP growth rate})i\text{-}1 \cdot (1\text{-Depreciation rate})j\text{-}I}$$

(i=1, 2, ..., j; j=total number of years of capital raising period)

⑥ Finally, starting with the calculated amount of X1 and increasing it annually according to the South's GDP growth rate, the goal of forming the desired level of physical capital will be achieved by the end of the income adjustment period.

Addendum: This portion corresponds to the costs associated with rapidly growing the North's economy to catch up with the South after reunification.

Realistically, in addition to this, the minimum subsistence level must be provided to northern residents during the initial chaotic period following reunification.

It is estimated that these two components can be covered by approximately 7% of the South's GDP over a 10-year period after reunification.

This is possible because measures will be taken to allow for separate management of the South and North for the first 10 years after reunification.

If the South and North were immediately integrated from the beginning of reunification, and northern residents demanded the same benefits as southern residents, the overall plan would become impossible. Therefore, all the aforementioned conditions must be met.

Conclusion

Let us all, Koreans around the world, join hands to create reunification and together live in peace and prosperity.

They say that one person's dream is just a dream, but everyone's dream becomes a reality.

Now, let us all break free from apathy towards reunification.

Just because we have defended ourselves under the guise of anti-communism, reunification will not come naturally. Nor will it come naturally just because we have lived peacefully. We must set a clear and direct goal for reunification itself. No one in this world, no matter where we look, will reunify us. We are the ones who must do it. If those who should do it sit idly by, nothing will happen. Neither the North Korean authorities are qualified nor their residents capable. Ultimately, it can only start with the people of the South.

It may seem convenient to ignore reunification and just live, but in fact, we have to live a difficult life while continuously paying enormous division costs. Eventually, we will become a miserable country. We must escape from this misfortune and bondage. Moreover, we cannot pass this on to our descendants generation after generation. We who are alive now must solve it.

Let's look squarely at our reality. We can fully afford the reunification cost. The sooner reunification happens, the less money it will cost. And reunification is actually an opportunity, not a burden. In fact, it's a daebak. The highest economic growth rate ever and the resulting abundance of jobs await us.

Even so, do you want to just be swept away by the trend of indifference and taboo towards reunification and just live carelessly? Let's all look at reality properly. Just because pro-North Korean forces are the only ones who loudly call for reunification, we should not turn a blind eye to reunification itself. In fact, pro-North Korean forces are not even qualified to mention it. We should ignore such people and look at reunification itself.

If we are determined to achieve reunification, knowing for sure that it is beneficial, what should we do and how? A military solution is out of the question. Political negotiations will not lead to a conclusion. Ultimately, we must pursue the path of economic superiority. Using our economic power, the best way to achieve reunification is to guide the North Korean people onto the right path. Let's firmly instill in them the dream of a reunification daebak that we will create together.

As long as the hearts of the North Korean people are tied to the Kim dynasty, the North Korean regime will not easily collapse, even after 40 or 50 years. Let's stop daydreaming about reunification happening suddenly one day. Let's conceptually separate the North Korean ruling group centered around the Kim family from the general population, the oppressed class. And let's help them in a way that reaches the North Korean people at their level. In this way, we can build trust while conveying the sincerity of South Koreans that we are one. If there are any benefits to the North Korean authorities in the process, let us resolve such issues with our solid defense capabilities. It would be foolish to lose sight of the main goal by worrying about trivial matters.

The hearts of the people are the will of heaven. Let us do our utmost with all our sincerity. Eventually, heaven will answer this nation. When reunification is achieved, let us move on to the desirable process of successfully completing the reunification process. However, without specifics to carry out this goal, no matter how strong our sense of purpose, it is all an illusion. In this sense, there are the most important parts that we must keep in mind to successfully complete reunification. These are the crucial conditions for reunification that I have explained earlier.

First, for 10 years after reunification, the South and North will be managed separately in terms of economics. Second, for 10 years after reunification, all physical capital invested in the North will be produced and supplied by the South, except in cases where clear problems arise, implementing a "Buy Korean Products" policy. Third, for 10 years after reunification, military spending can be kept at 1% of GDP. In the process of pursuing this structure, seasoned diplomacy must be supported to prevent any disruptions to the latter two. And fourth, instead of returning physical property to the original owners of land and real estate in the North, they will be compensated with land certificates. It is desirable for the land compensation system in both the South and North to follow the same trend as the land reform under the Rhee Syng-man government just before the Korean War. While maintaining state ownership of land in the North, it would be desirable to unify the land system in the South into state ownership in the long term, fundamentally eliminating land speculation, a malignant existence in the market economy system. I hope that our future generations will solve this issue rationally over a long period of time.

If all the institutional reunification work is completed after 10 years of reunification, then 10 years after, the entire unified Korea will become the second largest economy in the world, right after the United States. Unified Korea will be ahead of the United Kingdom, Germany, France, and Japan. We, the South and North

Korean people, can live a stable life with dignity in a strong country. Also, each of us can be proud of our descendants for generations to come.

Based on this, we can expand our ideology of Hongik Ingan throughout the world, following the flow of our people that has originated from Central Asia since ancient times.

Also, seeing the achievements we have made with all our efforts, many countries will follow the example of Unified Korea, which achieved the reunification daebak beyond the Miracle on the Han River, and dream of the K-dream in order to create a world where all people live well together. Thus, we expect to steadily play a leading role in the world of Hongik Ingan, our original noble ideology.

This may sound like a mere dream. However, if we all join hands and make up our minds, we can make this dream a reality. I look forward to a completely new history beginning for our nation.

Epilogue

The origin of the reunification daebak framework goes back to August 1992. I was commissioned by Peaceful Unification Advisory Council to estimate the reunification cost and presented the world's first comprehensive reunification cost estimate and its financing method.

The conclusion was that while the reunification cost would be substantial, we had the capacity to bear it. However, the media sensationalized only the absolute amount of the reunification cost on the front page, completely deviating from my intention. This led the public to develop an internal distance from reunification.

As this trend continued, a sentiment that reunification would be a burden became widespread among the people.

With such a biased perspective, reunification would be impossible. After much deliberation, in 2007, I posted a report titled "Reunification Costs and Benefits (2007)" on the National Assembly Budget Committee's homepage.

At that time, I advocated for a framework where South Korea alone would reap enormous benefits by adopting a "Buy Korean Products" policy. This framework was inspired by the fact that Japan had benefited greatly from the Korean War in the 1950s.

Later, in 2012, I compiled the results into a book and expressed this enormous benefit using the word "daebak".

It wasn't a perfectly fitting word, but there was no more suitable term, so I had to use a somewhat colloquial expression. In our thousands of years of history, there has never been such an incredibly good opportunity, so I couldn't find a suitable word for it. Through this process, the casually used term "daebak" has now become a common noun, and you can even find "daebak" in English dictionaries with the Korean pronunciation.

In her 2014 New Year's press conference, President Park Geun-hye stated, "Reunification is a daebak. I believe that..." This remark brought about a revolutionary shift in public sentiment. The percentage of citizens who believed reunification was necessary jumped from around 53% to a remarkable 82.6%, overcoming long-standing concerns about the financial burden of reunification. This laid the groundwork for significantly advancing the cause of reunification.

However, some people who were unaware of the details considered this a mere political slogan without concrete substance.

Since the publication of my book, "Reunification is a Daebak," in 2012, the concept of the reunification daebak and the reunification daebak framework have increasingly been recognized as an invaluable treasure that will elevate our nation to a glorious position on the world stage. It is not simply one of many reunification theories. When it becomes the dream and hope of us all, our nation will embark on a path to becoming the protagonist of a new history.

In recent years, foreign scholars, including those from the United States, have predicted that a unified Korea will become one of the world's two superpowers. I believe this is a reflection of the opinions of foreign scholars who have read the English version of my book "Reunification is a Daebak." It is not just a casual remark, but rather an assessment based on the book's theoretical and concrete simulations. Given that I am the only person in the world to propose a framework for reunification leading to a reunification daebak, I believe this is a contribution made by my English version of the book.

When the reunification daebak is achieved, almost all countries will look enviously at the progress of a unified Korea and aspire to a "K-Dream," a desire to become as successful as Korea.

Riding this wave, I anticipate a day when we will stand at the center of the world, realizing our people's original ideology of Hongik Ingan.

References

Shinn Chang-min, "Estimation of Reunification Costs between South and North Korea and Its Financing Plans," The Peaceful Unification Advisory Council, Icheon Conference, August 28, 1992.

Shinn Chang-min, "Conditions of Theory R," Shinn Chang-min's Reunification Column, Maeil Business Newspaper, December 13, 1994, p.27.

Shinn Chang-min, <Reunification Costs and Benefits (2007)>, National Assembly Budget Committee, Homepage, Publication No. 116, August 31, 2007.

Shinn Chang-min, <Reunification is a Daebak>, Maegyeong Publishing Co., July 16, 2012.

Shinn Chang-min, The Road to One Korea, Prosperity in Peace, (ed. Terence Murphy), Hanwoori Press, February 7, 2014.

Shinn Chang-min, <Reunification is a Daebak>, 6th edition, Hanwoori Reunification Publishing Co., October 3, 2015.

Shinn Chang-min, <Reunification Daebak is a Blessing>, 1st edition, Hanwoori Reunification Publishing Co., May 4, 2016.

Shinn Chang-min, <Reunification is a Daebak>, New edition, Hanwoori Reunification Publishing Co., March 15, 2017.

Shinn Chang-min, "Theory of Korean Unification Policy – Voluntary Reunification," pp. 28-31, 1st Seminar Room, National Assembly Member's Building, September 14, 2017.

Shinn Chang-min, "Conceptualizing a Special Law for Reunification Daebak," <Reunification Daebak Summary>, 5th Forum of Reunification Daebak Implementation Solidarity, May 3, 2024.

Shim Baek-gang, <China was Part of Korea in History>, Bareun History Publishing, August 26, 2021.

We are not pursuing a reunification that merely consumes natural resources in the North. We envision a reunification where North and South Koreans work together to create wealth!

Who would fear reunification due to its cost? Through the process of establishing physical capital in the North, we will all achieve tremendous economic growth.

In short, it will be a **Daebak**! **An extraordinary Daebak**! **A super-Daebak** for all citizens of a unified Republic of Korea, both North and South!

Let us relocate the Kim family regime to somewhere else and let us South and North Koreans join hands to live a prosperous life together!

Forever!!!

Long live the Republic of Korea!!!!!

Reunification Daebak!!!

About the Author Chang-min Shinn, Ph.D.

Professor Emeritus, Chung-Ang University, Soeul Korea

Chairman, Tongildaebak Association

Chairman, Hanwoori Reunification Research Institute

Chairman, Unified Economy Research Association

Dean, College of Business Administration, CAU

Claremont Graduate University, Ph.D. in economics

University of Southern California, MA in economics

College of Law, Seoul National University

Contact Information:

Phone: +82-10-9423-3399

Email: cms21@cau.ac.kr

www.unidaebak.com